I0605734

ENGINEERING ANSWERS

How Rockets Reach Space

BY ARNOLD RINGSTAD

Kids Core
An Imprint of Abdo Publishing
abdobooks.com

abdobooks.com

Published by Abdo Publishing, a division of ABDO, PO Box 398166, Minneapolis, Minnesota 55439.

Printed in the United States of America, North Mankato, Minnesota.
102024
012025

Cover Photo: Dima Zel/Shutterstock Images
Interior Photos: Red Huber/Getty Images News/Getty Images, 4–5; Kim Shiflett/NASA, 6; Terry White/SLS/NASA, 8; Kevin Dietsch/Getty Images News/Getty Images, 10; blickwinkel/McPhoto/MDF/Alamy, 12–13; Jude Guidry/NASA, 14; Kenny Allen/NASA, 16; Randy Beaudoin/NASA, 18; Koichi Wakata/NASA, 20–21; Bill Ingalls/NASA, 22; NASA, 25; Planetpix/Alamy Live News/SpaceX/Alamy, 26; Austin Lowery/NASA, 28; Jack Pfaller/NASA, 29 (top); Konstantin Shaklein/Alamy, 29 (bottom)

Editor: Marley Richmond
Series Designer: Laura Kuchar

Library of Congress Control Number: 2024938385

Publisher's Cataloging-in-Publication Data

Names: Ringstad, Arnold, author.
Title: How rockets reach space / by Arnold Ringstad
Description: Minneapolis, Minnesota: ABDO Publishing, 2025 | Series: Engineering answers | Includes online resources and index.
Identifiers: ISBN 9781098295882 (lib. bdg.) | ISBN 9798384916888 (ebook)
Subjects: LCSH: Engineering--Juvenile literature. | Rockets (Aeronautics)--Juvenile literature. | Outer Space--Juvenile literature. | Space vehicles--Juvenile literature. | Questions and answers--Juvenile literature. | Engineering design--Juvenile literature.
Classification: DDC 620.1--dc23

CONTENTS

NASA's first successful test of the Space Launch System began on November 16, 2022.

CHAPTER 1

Blast Off!

Spotlights shine on a huge rocket. The Space Launch System (SLS) sits on a launchpad in Florida. **Engineers** prepare it for launch.

SLS stands 322 feet (98 m) tall. A white spacecraft is at the top of the rocket. Below that is SLS's orange center section.

Each of SLS's boosters is too large to move in one piece. Engineers stack five pieces together to create each booster near the launchpad.

This is called the core stage. It holds large tanks of **propellant**. At the base of the core stage are four engines. On the sides are two white boosters. The engines and boosters will soon send SLS to space.

The engineers count down. With a few seconds left, the four engines fire. Flames shoot downward. When the count reaches zero, the boosters fire. More flames cover the launchpad. The rocket blasts off into the night sky.

SLS zooms upward. It also begins to tilt. The rocket is headed to **orbit**. To do this, it must build a lot of speed and eventually turn sideways. About two minutes after launch, the boosters separate from the rocket. They have used up their propellant. The boosters fall back to Earth.

Artemis Program

SLS is an important part of the Artemis program. This program plans to land **astronauts** on the Moon. SLS will launch the astronauts into space. Then the astronauts will use a separate vehicle for the Moon landing.

Space Launch System

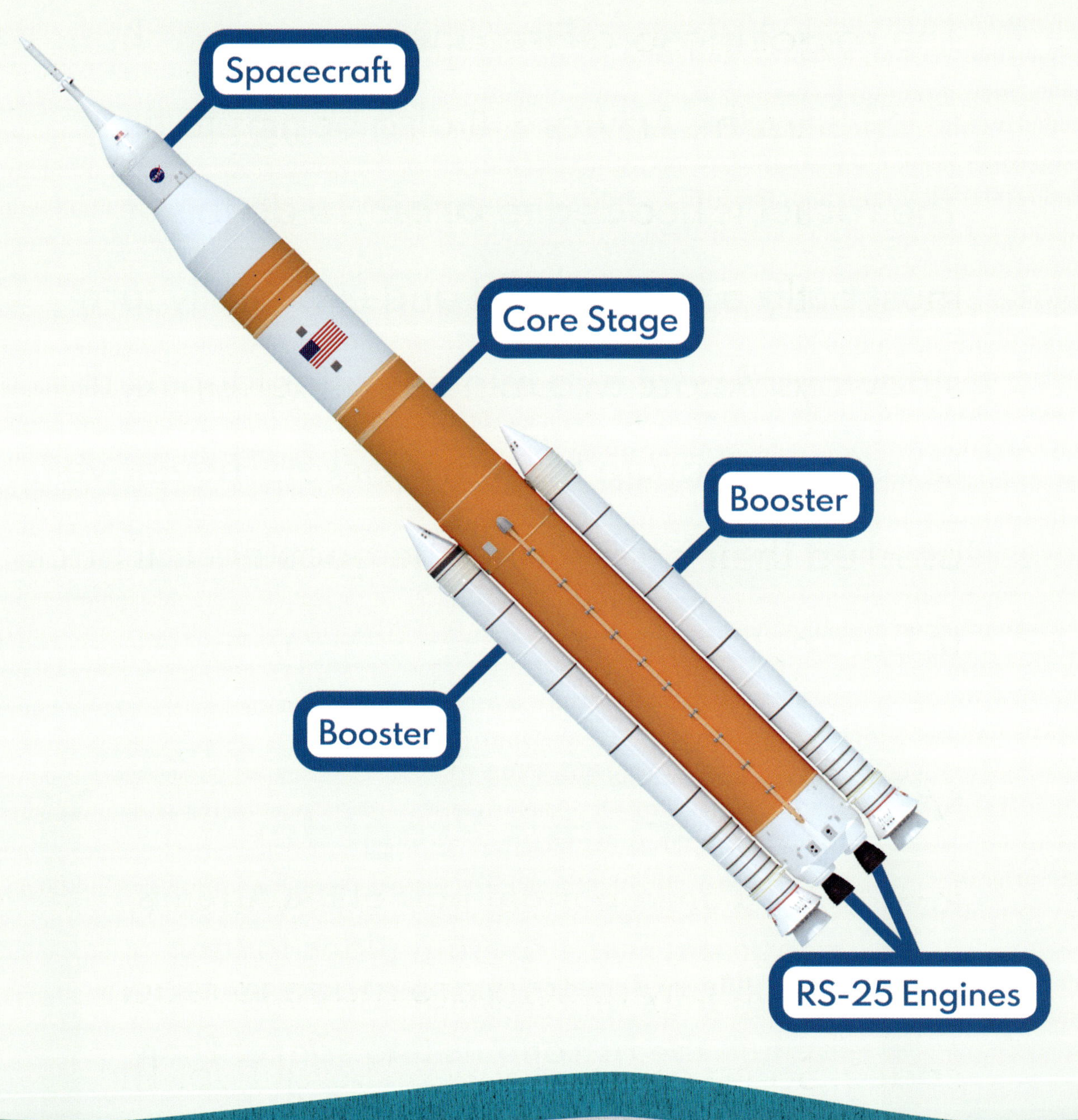

The SLS is made of many parts. Each one serves a purpose to get the rocket into orbit.

The rest of the rocket continues to space. It is now going more than 3,000 miles per hour (4,800 km/h). And it is still speeding up.

About eight and a half minutes after launch, the four engines shut down. The core stage's tanks are empty. This part of the rocket separates. The white spacecraft continues onward to orbit. It is now going more than 17,000 miles per hour (27,400 km/h).

What Are Rockets?

Rockets are vehicles that use a powerful type of engine. Many rockets are made to reach space. Some rockets launch straight up. They reach space for a short time. Then they fall back down to Earth. Other rockets launch into orbit.

New types of rockets are being developed. The company SpaceX makes the Falcon 9 rocket. It is reusable.

They circle Earth and can stay in space for a long time.

The first rocket to reach orbit launched in 1957. Since then, thousands of rockets have reached space. Some launch **satellites** into orbit. Others send spacecraft to distant planets. Rockets also carry **astronauts** into space.

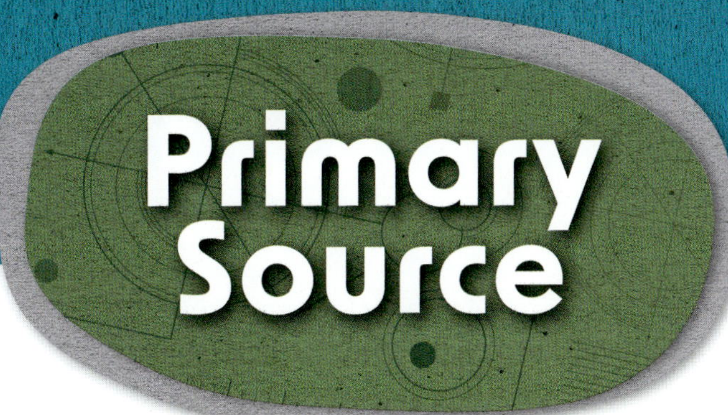

Charlie Blackwell-Thompson is a launch director for SLS. She said:

> The most exciting part of this job overall is launch day. You work for years and months and weeks . . . to move toward a goal. That goal is a safe and successful launch at the beginning of a mission.

Source: Sascha Medina. "It's America's Rocket." *NC Space Grant*, 6 Apr. 2023, ncspacegrant.ncsu.edu. Accessed 28 Dec. 2023.

What's the Big Idea?

Read this quote carefully. What is its main idea? Explain how the main idea is supported by details.

The heavier a rocket is, the more thrust its engines must produce to take off.

CHAPTER 2

Powering a Rocket

Rockets work by burning propellant to create hot gas. This gas shoots out the back of the engine. It goes through a part of the engine called a **nozzle**. This creates a force called thrust that pushes the rocket forward.

SLS uses fuel tanks that hold 196,000 gallons (742,000 L) of liquid oxygen.

Rocket propellant is made up of two parts. The first part is fuel. This is a substance that burns when combined with oxygen. The second part is oxidizer. This is a substance that contains oxygen. Burning fuel and oxidizer releases hot gas to create powerful thrust.

Solid or Liquid?

Some propellants are in liquid form. SLS uses hydrogen for its liquid fuel. The oxidizer is usually liquid oxygen.

Keeping Propellants Cold

Many liquid propellants must be kept very cold to stay in liquid form. For example, liquid oxygen is stored at −297 degrees Fahrenheit (−183°C). Liquid hydrogen is stored at −423 degrees Fahrenheit (−253°C). Tanks are specially built to keep the propellants cold.

NASA's space shuttle program ran from 1981 to 2011. The space shuttle's rocket used a large orange fuel tank on the outside of the rocket.

Liquid propellant is stored in tanks on the rocket. Pipes and pumps move it down to the engines. Inside the engines, the fuel and oxidizer mix. A spark often starts the burning process.

Propellants also come in solid form. In these rockets, fuel and oxidizer are combined in a solid substance. This material is packed into a casing with a nozzle at the bottom. When the engine is lit, the solid propellant burns.

Rockets may use both solid and liquid propellants. SLS is an example of this. The four engines in the center section burn liquid propellant. The white boosters on the sides use solid propellant. Together, they create the thrust that sends the rocket into space.

Steering a Rocket

Rockets must point in the right direction to reach orbit. They have to keep flying straight and steady. Engineers create computer programs that steer rockets. Rockets have a few ways to steer.

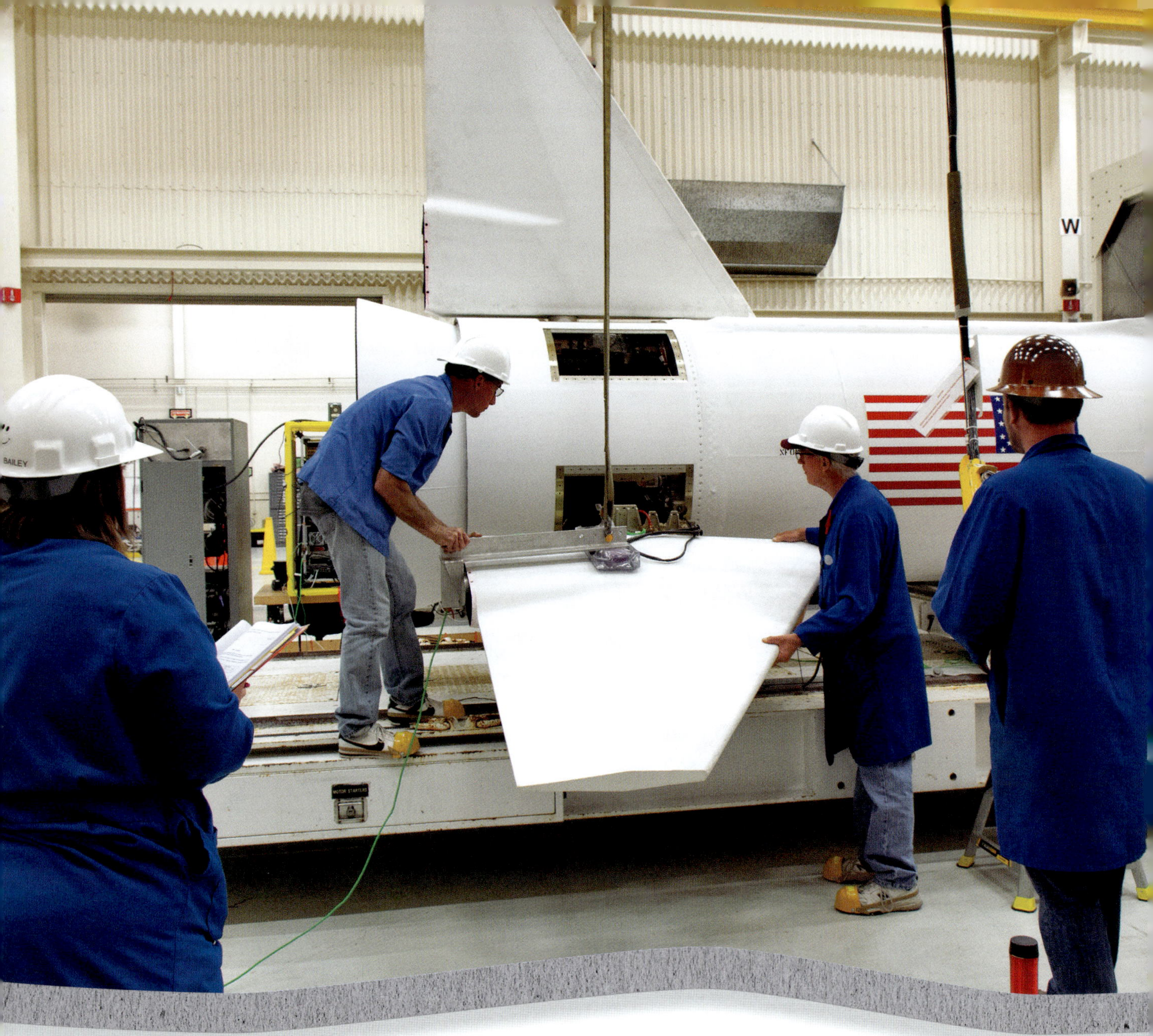

Engineers install fins on rockets to prepare them for launch.

The first way is to use fins. These work like the wings on an airplane. Air flows over the fins. This helps keep the rocket stable. Moving the fins can steer the rocket. However, fins need air. As the rocket flies higher, the air around it becomes thinner. Fins stop working.

The second way to steer is to use engines that can tilt. Pointing the engine's nozzle in one direction turns the rocket that direction. Small tilting movements steer the rocket and keep it steady. Engines do not need air, unlike fins.

Explore Online

Visit the website below. Does it give any new information about rockets that wasn't in Chapter Two?

What Is a Rocket?

abdocorelibrary.com/rockets-reach-space

The International Space Station (ISS) is in Earth's orbit. Rockets take astronauts there. On the ISS, astronauts experience weightlessness.

CHAPTER 3

Fighting Gravity

Gravity pulls objects toward the ground. People work against gravity in daily life. Simply standing up requires fighting gravity. So does shooting a basketball. Rockets must overcome gravity too.

The Soyuz rocket generates more than 900,000 pounds (408,000 kg) of thrust to take off.

A rocket's thrust needs to be stronger than the pull of gravity. This allows the rocket to lift off the launchpad. The rocket continues creating thrust to keep rising.

To reach space, a rocket travels through the **atmosphere**. In addition to gravity, it must fight another force. Air in the atmosphere pushes against the flying rocket. This creates a force called drag. The air becomes thinner as the rocket rises. Thin air creates less drag.

Where Does Space Begin?

There is no clear division between the atmosphere and space. However, many scientists mark the beginning of space at 62 miles (100 km) from Earth's surface. The air is very thin above this point.

Stages to Space

Rockets must fire their engines for several minutes to reach space. This requires a lot of propellant. Rockets drop their heavy tanks once they are empty. Dropping empty tanks means rockets use less fuel on each trip. They can carry heavier **payloads**.

Engineers build rockets in sections. These sections are called stages. The lowest part of the rocket is the first stage. This stage fires its engines to lift off the ground. It pushes the rocket through the atmosphere. Then it runs out of propellant. The first stage falls away.

The next part of the rocket is the second stage. It has its own propellant tanks. It has at least one engine. After the first stage falls away,

After rocket stages fall away, many of them remain in space and orbit Earth.

the second stage fires up. The rocket continues to space.

Many rocket designs use stages. The Saturn V rocket launched astronauts to the Moon. It used three stages. The Falcon 9 launches astronauts and satellites today. It uses two stages.

The first stage of a Falcon 9 rocket is designed to land back on Earth after it separates. This stage can then be reused.

Rockets that reach space are complex and expensive. Engineers work hard to make them reliable. They test rockets before using them for important missions. Launching rockets always carries some risk. But engineers make sure reaching space is as safe as possible.

Further Evidence

Look at the website below. Does it give any new evidence to support Chapter Three?

How Do We Launch Things into Space?

abdocorelibrary.com/rockets-reach-space

Engineering Facts

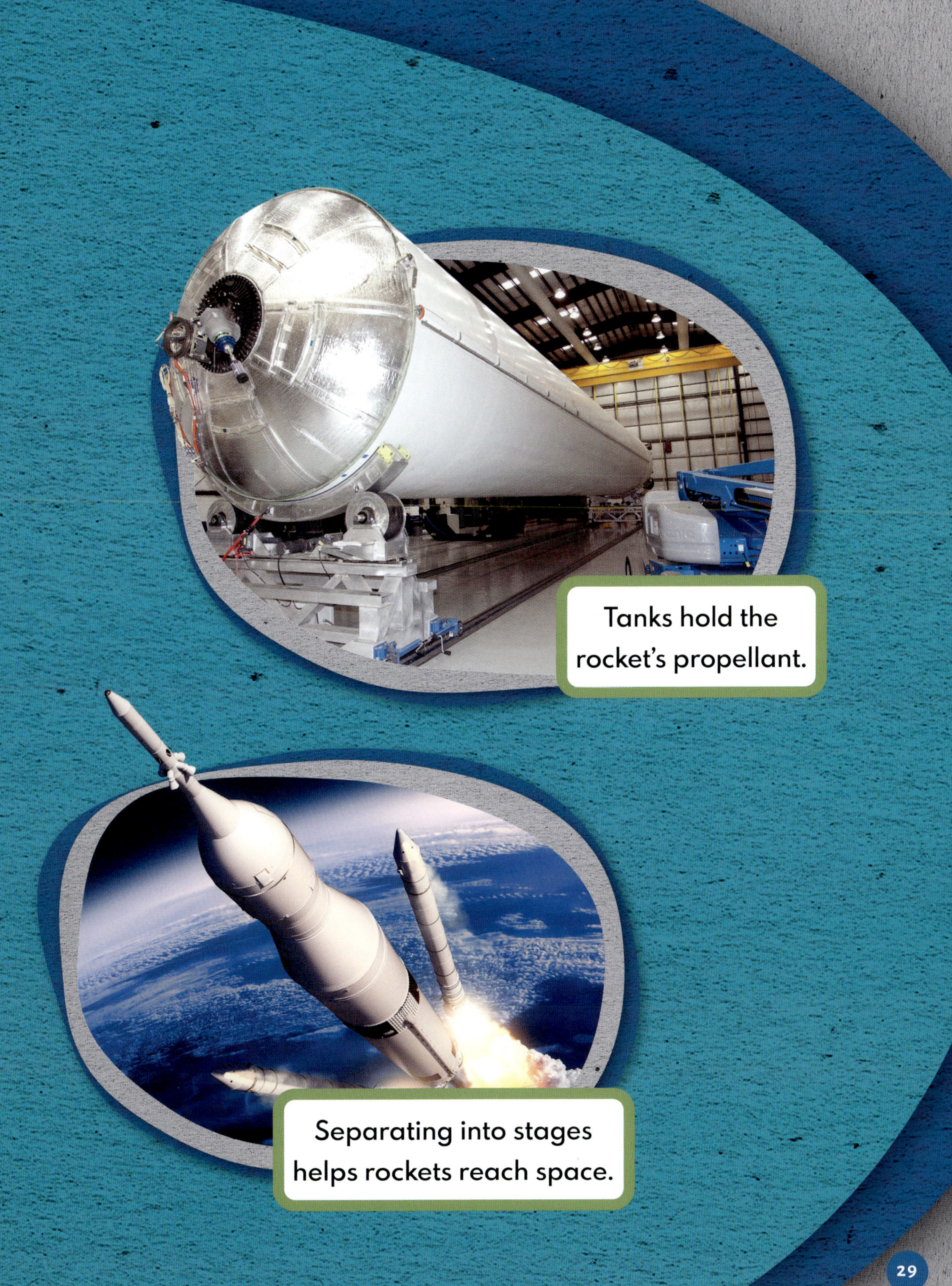
Tanks hold the rocket's propellant.

Separating into stages helps rockets reach space.

Glossary

astronauts
people who travel into space

atmosphere
the layers of gases that surround Earth

engineers
people who are trained to design and build machines and structures

nozzle
the part of a rocket engine where hot gases shoot out

orbit
a path in space that one object takes around another

payloads
objects that a rocket carries into space

propellant
the materials that are combined and burned to create thrust, including fuel and oxidizer

satellites
objects that are in orbit

Online Resources

To learn more about rockets, visit our free resource websites below.

Visit **abdocorelibrary.com** or scan this QR code for free Common Core resources for teachers and students, including vetted activities, multimedia, and booklinks, for deeper subject comprehension.

Visit **abdobooklinks.com** or scan this QR code for free additional online weblinks for further learning. These links are routinely monitored and updated to provide the most current information available.

Learn More

Gagliardi, Sue. *Cardboard Rocket Challenge!* Abdo, 2021.

Gater, Will. *The Mysteries of the Universe*. DK, 2020.

Murray, Julie. *SpaceX*. Abdo, 2022.

Index

About the Author

Arnold Ringstad is a writer and editor in Minnesota. He enjoys learning about space exploration.